Jackie Bushman's Top 50 Whitetail Tactics

Hunting techniques that really work

Jackie Bushman

The Lyons Press

Guilford, Connecticut
An imprint of The Globe Pequot Press

Copyright © 2002 by Jackie Bushman

First Lyons Press paperback edition, 2006

The Lyons Press is an imprint of The Globe Pequot Press.

10 9 8 7 6 5 4 3 2

Printed in the United States of America

ISBN 978-1-59228-925-7

Library of Congress Cataloging-in-Publication Data is available on file.

Dedication

This book is dedicated to my father, Jack C. Bushman, a former world-class tennis pro and coach and later a successful insurance salesman. His belief that "when you think you've gotten too good you'll never get any better" is something I've always kept in mind.

I also thank him for introducing me to his good friend, the late Perry Mendel, the founder and chairman of KinderCare. Mr. Mendel was a true visionary and the best business coach anyone could ever ask for. In addition to putting up the seed money for Buckmasters, he took me under his wing and gave me a business education that was second to none.

Without the dedication of these two men and their belief in me, Buckmasters would not be here. I thank them both and dedicate this book to them.

Contents

Introduction   xi

1 Keep The Faith   1
You never know when a bad hunting season will turn good

2 Back To The Basics   4
Focus on basic whitetail knowledge and hunting skills

3 Identifying Food Sources   7
Learn what deer eat and the game is half won

4 Aerial Photos   10
How to find and use aerial photos of your hunting spot

5 Know Your Property   13
The deer know the lay of the land and so should you

6 Trailing for Deer   16
Learn how whitetails use their freeways

7 Water and Fences   19
Two hunting spots that are easy to locate

8 Bottlenecks or Funnels   22
Use the terrain to bring deer to you

9 Walking Silently   25
Slow down; you move too fast

10 Tracks and Droppings   28
Identify and interpret key whitetail sign

11 Finding Rubs   31
Locate a buck's signpost

12 Breeding Scrapes   34
How dominant bucks seek female companionship

13 Looking For Deer In All The Wrong Places   37
Adjust your viewpoint to see more whitetails

14 Whitetail Body Language   40
Learn to read a deer's mood

15 Take A Stand   43
Learn the most effective technique for whitetails

CONTENTS

16   Treestand Strategy 46
Look for the perfect ambush spot

17   Spot and Stalk 49
Locate a buck in the distance and get close enough for the shot

18   The Rut 52
This is one time when mature bucks throw caution to the wind

19   The Grunt Stop 55
Make the deer stop where you want him.

20   Antler Rattling 58
When and how this controversial technique works best

21   Nose of The Whitetail 61
Defeat a deer's first line of defense

22   People Stink 64
Overcome human odor and avoid spooking deer

23   Silent Drives 67
Make deer move when they don't want to

24   Clothes Make The Deer Hunter 70
Dress for success

25   Gizmos 73
Accessories that help bring home the buck

26   Backpacks 76
Use one to organize your gear

27   Ammunition 79
Selection has never been better

28   Ballistics 82
Understand your ammunition

29   Binoculars 85
All deer hunters need these bionic eyes

30   Rangefinders 88
Take the guesswork out of short- or long-range shots

31   Scope It Out 91
Use a scope sight for precise bullet placement

32   Guns and Bows 94
Choose what's right for your hunting style

33   Sighting In 97
Make sure your gun shoots where it's supposed to shoot

CONTENTS

34 Fighting The Flinch   100
Avoid this common shooting problem

35 Perfect Practice Makes Perfect   103
Good bucks are seldom shot at the rifle range

36 Give It a Rest   106
Here's the key to accurate shooting

37 The Perfect Shot   109
Learn whitetail anatomy and where to aim

38 Don't Miss High   112
Concentrate to avoid shooting over your trophy

39 Medicine for Buck Fever   115
Control the disease but don't cure it

40 Looking for The Eyes   118
Don't move when the deer can see you

41 Archery Mechanics   121
Use these tips to shoot a straight arrow

42 Peak Deer Movement   124
If you can't hunt all day, hunt early and late

43 Be A Weather Watcher   127
Predict how weather changes affect deer movement

44 Mooning for Bucks   130
Hunt midday during a full moon

45 After The Shot   133
Follow up every shot taken at a deer

46 Approaching Fallen Deer   136
Are the eyes open or closed?

47 Shots For a Lifetime   139
Spend time, thought, and film to photograph your prize

48 Work Just Begins   142
Field work is important in making wild game tasty

49 Safety Sense   145
Treat all guns like they're loaded

50 More Safety Sense   148
File a game plan when you head for the deer woods

Introduction

In writing this book, there are a few people to thank. The first is my dad, because he got me started in athletics. He instilled in me the desire to win and the determination to be the best. The most important thing Dad taught me was that no matter what sport you are playing, you have to have your fundamentals down if you want to succeed. I saw this through my junior years in tennis and basketball all the way through my collegiate and professional years of tennis. You are only as good as your basics, your foundation.

Once you have a firm grasp of the basics, commitment and practice will determine how good you will become. This concept was true for me when I started deer hunting. It took me years to figure out that I did not have a firm grasp of deer hunting basics. I had to regroup and return to my early days of sports to get going. Once I got going, the light came on and my success for taking good bucks began.

After I stopped playing professional tennis, I taught the sport for 12 years. Again, this is something I wanted to be the best at. Many great players are not good teachers because they cannot communicate in simple terms. Whether teaching a child or an adult, you must present the lesson in a way the student can understand. Keep it simple.

The same concept applies to deer hunting. This is not rocket science, but you are dealing with ego, and that can be the biggest obstacle.

My main purpose in doing this book is to help others experience the emotion of taking a good buck. If you are a beginner, these tips will get you on the right track. If you're like I was and have been hunting for years with no luck, I hope these tips make your dream come true.

Another person I would like to recognize is my late grandfather John Walraven. Better known as Poppy, he got me involved in hunting and fishing. The many days we spent in the field strengthened my love of the outdoors. He taught me gun safety and respect for the animals we hunt.

In reading this book, ask yourself: "Am I solid in deer hunting basics?" Be honest, drop your ego, and get to work. Become a student of the game and never think you are too good to learn something new. You are hunting the number one game animal in the world. You will learn respect for this animal because you will lose to him more often than you will win. When hard work, time, and effort pay off with a dream buck, the result is a lifetime memory.

My father and grandfather taught me a lot about sports and hunting, but if we are lucky, all of us have mentors in our professional careers, too. Mine was Perry Mendel, the founder of KinderCare. Mr. Mendel was not a deer hunter, but he believed in Buckmasters and he taught me valuable business lessons that helped make Buckmasters a success. One of the most important things he taught me was to look at the big picture; to not let myself get so caught up in the details that I forgot to see where I was going and why.

Sometimes, we forget the big picture in hunting. All of us get a thrill out of outsmarting deer or taking a trophy. But, more than that, hunting is about discovery. It's about learning as much as we can about this fascinating animal called the whitetail deer, and it's about the great outdoors. It's about enjoying the sunrises and watching the woods wake up in the morning and sharing all of that with friends old and new. Learn the basics, but never forget the big picture.

Good luck and safe hunting.

—Jackie Bushman
November 1, 2001

1

Keep The Faith

When I tell people that I get out of a warm bed well before daylight and sit 25 feet up a tree in freezing temperatures, they tell me I'm crazy. Actually, I'm just in love with the outdoors and deer hunting. What is it about white-tailed deer that makes millions of hunters pursue them?

Whitetails are amazing animals. A lot of hunters arc recognized as "experts" on whitetails, but I don't think anybody is really an expert. Even the so-called experts get outsmarted by the deer much more often than not. In fact, there's no game animal in North America that more consistently defeats the hunter. There are more than 20 million deer in North America, and hunters take three to four million a season. You tell me who's winning. Deer will thrive in your suburban backyard and eat your ornamental bushes, or they'll thrive in remote areas where they rarely see a human.

No matter where whitetails are hunted, most people are unlikely to see them; at least, they don't see the mature bucks that represent deer hunting's ultimate goal. It's those mature bucks that grow the biggest antlers, and it's those antlers that capture our imagination. Whitetail antlers are as unique as human fingerprints. They're all similar, but no two sets of deer antlers are exactly alike.

When you finally put all the pieces of the deer hunting puzzle together, you'll get a feeling like nothing you've ever experienced before. I want every deer hunter who's willing to do the homework and study the game to feel the elation that I've been blessed to feel in my lifetime.

No deer hunter succeeds every time. The idea is to be consistently successful. We've all heard stories about the first-time deer hunter who did everything wrong and still shot the Boone and Crockett buck. Those stories keep us going when the hunting gets slow. Here's a good tip to remember: Don't ever lose faith. It only takes about 30 seconds for a deer season to go from bad to good.

Always keep the faith—you never know when a big bruiser like this is going to show up. *Credit: George Barnett*

2

Back
To The Basics

If you've been deer hunting for a long time and you've never taken a mature buck, maybe it's time to focus on fundamentals. When I coached tennis, I made sure my students understood the game's fundamentals. In the excitement of a match, they sometimes forgot the basics and their game suffered because of it. It's the same with deer hunting.

If you're not successful, you need to get back to the basics. Deer hunting isn't rocket science; it's really very simple. What do the deer eat? Where do the deer bed and where do they travel? When do they move most often? Where do you

What do deer eat? Where do they bed? Find the answers to these two basic questions, and your odds for success will increase remarkably. *Credit: Ray Sasser*

set up or select a stand to intercept them? How do you defeat the whitetail's sensory defenses—smell, hearing, and sight? How do you read sign to know that you're hunting in a productive area? How do you reach your hunting area without alerting nearby deer? When is the rut?

I was always a good athlete and I've always had a competitive nature. When I started seriously hunting whitetails, I worked hard and put in lots of time, but I just wasn't getting the job done. It's tough to admit that you're a poor deer hunter, but that's what I was. So I approached deer hunting as if it were tennis. I went back to school. I found hunters who were successful and I learned from them. My brain became a sponge to soak up deer hunting knowledge. To improve, you have to drop your ego, which is something else I learned from tennis. In fact as a coach, I'd much rather teach someone who's never played and has no preconceived notions about their abilities, than teach someone who has already developed a lot of bad habits and refuses to admit it.

We all have room for improvement. I learn something new about whitetails every season. There are times when it seems like I learn something new nearly every day of the season. One of my father's favorite sayings is this one: "When you think you've gotten too good, you'll never get any better." One of the most important tips I can give you is drop your ego and concentrate on the fundamentals.

3

Identifying Food Sources

One of the indisputable facts about deer hunting is that deer have to eat in order to survive. Because of this, it's critical that you know what food sources are prevalent in your part of the country. When you go in the woods, for example, know what a white oak acorn looks like. Know what the white oak bark and leaves look like, because you'll be scouting before or after the season when acorns are hard to find. Where white oaks exist, their acorns are like ice cream to a deer because they have less tannic acid and are sweeter than other acorns.

Food sources change with the season. Find an area with a good white acorn crop, however, and you've found a deer candy store. *Credit: R. Thornberry*

Most deer hunters are not botanists, and neither am I, but you need to learn favorite food sources wherever you hunt. You can start by contacting the landowners or outfitters with whom you hunt. Those guys should know what their deer are eating. If you hunt public lands, call state, forest service, and soil-conservation-service biologists in your hunting area. It's their job to know what the wildlife eats. You can also go to a bookstore or go on-line and find regional plant identification books. Finally, check with your state game department, as many publish books or pamphlets that identify important plants.

Food sources change with the seasons, and you have to keep up with the trend. Many hunters go to the hardwoods on opening day, see deer everywhere, and then stay in the same stand all season. But once the acorns are gone, the deer move to alternate food sources. You have to adapt to the changing situations.

Pay attention to weather conditions, especially extreme ones such as a severe drought or harsh winter. These factors affect what food sources will be available from year to year. Don't take for granted that what happened last year will happen every year. For example, oak trees don't produce acorns every year. Go out in early fall and see for yourself which trees are loaded with acorns.

4

Aerial Photos

When I'm scouting or hunting a piece of property, my bible is a recent aerial photo. Aerial photos are available from the U.S. Geological Survey (USGS) for as little as $10. The Internet makes it easy to get aerial photos for your hunting area. Just go to the USGS site and you'll find all the information you need for buying them.

An aerial photo shows me the relationship between fields, creeks, hardwoods, bottlenecks, clear-cuts, fencelines, and ponds. I look for the dense cover (where the deer are most likely to bed), food sources, and the transition zones between feeding and bedding areas.

The photo also tells me compass directions, and lets me mark all my stand locations, the deer trails, and the best

Aerial photos like this can help you learn a piece of property in a hurry. Use photos in conjunction with topo maps.

approaches to the stands. There's not a morning that I go deer hunting that I don't watch the Weather Channel or try to otherwise find a forecast for that day. My stand selection is never determined until I see the weather forecast. You've got to have the wind in your favor. Wind direction is the single most critical aspect of deer hunting. If you know from the forecast that the wind direction is expected to change during the hunt, that's another factor in stand selection.

Not only is wind direction important in stand selection; it's also critical in how you approach the stand. You have to get to that stand without alarming deer that may be bedded or feeding nearby. That's where the aerial photo comes in. On my hunting lease in Alabama, for example, I have 40 different setups I can hunt. Looking at the aerial photo, I know the likely feeding areas, I know the likely bedding areas, and I know my stand locations and the approaches to all of them. Once I know the wind direction, I use that knowledge to select the ideal stand and to approach it without spooking deer.

In my early days, I had my stand location picked out the night before a hunt. I didn't consider wind direction. Boy, did I waste a lot of time on stands with the wrong wind direction. Don't get caught up in this trap. A buck's nose is his main defense. Don't try to fight it.

5

Know Your Property

Once you learn the food sources and have an aerial photo of your hunting spot, then it's time to walk the property. Treat your hunting property like it's your house. You want to know every inch of it. While walking the property, look for the various food sources that you've studied and learned to identify.

If that food is available, look for deer tracks, fresh droppings, empty hulls of acorns, or fresh bite marks where deer have nipped weeds, leaves, or other browse. Deer hunting is like taking a course at school. The more you learn about the deer's behavior, the better you'll be as a student of the game.

I've made it my business to learn every inch of the properties where I do most of my hunting. I hunt spring turkeys on the same places I deer hunt. I've learned a lot by walking in the spring when I'm not concerned about spooking a wary buck. You'll find where rubs and scrapes were and you might even find some shed antlers that tell you where a big old buck was hanging out.

You can't spend too much time in the woods. Right after the deer season, I'll go for walks and find new sign and maybe a feature of the land I didn't know was there. I can't tell you how many deer I've taken by finding new places on pieces of property I've been hunting for years. While you're scouting, keep your eyes open. Hunting is different from simply walking in the woods, and you never know when you'll see some clue that helps you find a buck.

If you're hunting on private property, you might use these scouting trips to put up markers that help you find stands easier. On our club property, we mark all the boundaries with different colored paint. We mark the northern boundary with blue paint. If our kids get lost and see the blue paint, they know which way to turn and get back to camp. That's another benefit of thoroughly walking the hunting area and paying attention to the terrain. It keeps you from getting lost.

Mentally, I want you to think that you're that old buck and someone is out to get you. Keep your house in mind. Do you think he's going to be sitting in the wide open living room or hiding in a corner of the attic?

Put yourself in the buck's shoes. You're that old buck, and you know someone is out to get you. *Credit: Jack Brock*

6

Trailing for Deer

Once you've located deer trails, look for tracks in the trails. If all the tracks are going in the same direction, follow the trail to determine where it goes. Depending on where the food source is, you may have found the main trail heading for the food source. It's helpful to know how far deer are traveling from the bedding area to the food source.

Deer sometimes enter a food source on one trail and leave on another. Other trails may be used both as entry and exit routes. You can study the tracks to determine what kind of trail you've found. Deer may enter a field, like a wheat field or sorghum field, on one trail, feed through the field, then go out on a different trail. They often use some trails in the morning and others in the afternoon.

A big buck moving down a trail. Find a major trail leading from bedding to feeding areas, and you've found a place to put your stand.
Credit: R. Thornberry

If you're hunting a field, set up in the morning on a trail the deer are using to travel from the field back to the bedding area. In the afternoon, set up on a trail deer are using to travel from the bedding area to the field.

When hunting pressure gets heavy, it's good to know where the deer are bedding, as they become nocturnal when they're heavily hunted. If you hunt a morning stand near a food source, the deer may leave the field and be past your stand before daylight. If you hunt an afternoon stand near the food source, they may not come out into the field until it's dark.

If you set up near the bedding area, you've got a better chance to see morning movement back to the bedding area at first light. You've also got a better chance to see an afternoon buck moving toward the food source while it's still daylight. If I can find two or three trails that merge into one trail, I know I've discovered a great place to put a stand.

Years ago, I used to spend my deer seasons sitting on the edges of fields in the afternoon. The first few days of each season the deer, including the bucks, would come to the fields with plenty of daylight left. Once we shot on the fields, however, we would never see the bucks again during shooting hours. At the time, I didn't have the confidence to take a trail back toward the bedding area and set up a stand. When I finally did, I lost visibility, but the sign back toward the bedding area let me know that I had made the right move. When pressured, most bucks will turn nocturnal, so you *have* to get closer to the bedding areas.

7

Water and Fences

Deer don't have to drink water every day to survive, but they will drink regularly if water is convenient. Water is particularly important to whitetails in the South and Southwest, where it may be hot during deer season, and in the West where water sources tend to be scarce.

For the hunter, water is less important where it's abundant. If there's a creek winding through your hunting area, the deer can drink anywhere along that creek. The fewer water sources the deer have, however, the more important water becomes as a stand site. By reading tracks around the waterhole

19

A whitetail at a waterhole. Find the trails leading to the waterhole, then set up your stand accordingly. *Credit: Ray Sasser*

and finding which trails are most active, you can determine how to set up. In dry areas, the waterholes may create a food source, with weeds and other browse growing up around the edges.

Fences are common in many deer hunting areas. It's easy to find popular crossings. Deer cross fences by ducking under or jumping over and, either way, tend to leave hair on the wire or wood. Where they duck under, deer will wallow out a distinct depression and kill the vegetation under the fence. The approaching trail to a heavily used fence crossing is also easy to see. Deer leave brown hair from their backs where they duck under a fence. Don't mistake cattle or feral hog hair for deer hair. Hair from hogs or cattle is coarser than deer hair. I'll remove the hair from a fence crossing, then check that spot a couple of days later. That gives me an idea of how frequently deer are using the crossing.

Where deer jump fences, they frequently leave white belly hair on the wire. Whitetails can jump much higher than a standard four-foot fence, but they're as lazy as people and only jump as high as necessary to clear the fence.

It's sometimes not a good idea to hunt crossings on a boundary fence between properties. If you shoot a deer as it crosses onto your property and it runs back the way it came, the neighbors may think you shot the deer on their side of the fence.

8

Bottlenecks or Funnels

Whenever I'm studying aerial photos or scouting the woods, I look for bottlenecks. A bottleneck acts like a funnel, and is a natural or man-made contour that the deer like to follow. A perfect example is a point of woods that extends across an open field. Whitetails like to stay in the cover as much as possible. Rather than cross the wide-open field, they'll stick to the woods where it narrows down. And that is a perfect place for a deer stand.

When I'm scouting, I look for connecting woodlots and wooded creek bottoms that cut through the open. White-

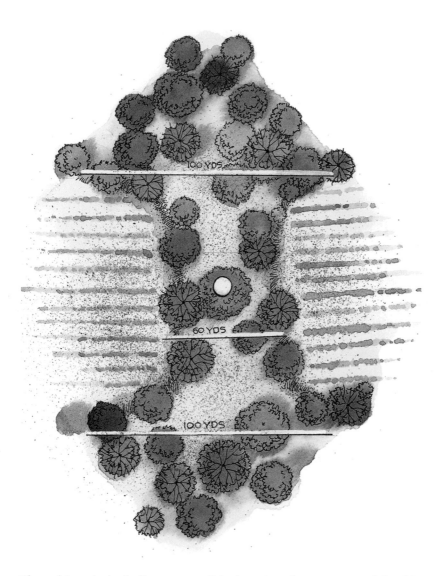

The white circle indicates possible location for a treestand in this wooded bottleneck. *Credit: Chris Armstrong*

tails use those places to move around undetected, and you'll usually find a lot of trails associated with them. If I'm bowhunting, I'll try to find a good stand tree in the middle of a bottleneck. When you set up in the middle, the odds are better that deer passing on either side of the stand will be in bow range. When hunting with firearms, you've got more latitude to play the wind and still have the deer pass in range. That all depends on visibility and the density of the cover.

I've taken a lot of good bucks by hunting bottlenecks. I was hunting in Canada on a full moon once, and the deer just weren't moving. The farmer happened to mention that he was driving around to check some cows and, because we knew the lay of the land, we knew he would drive upwind of a woodlot that bottlenecked into another woodlot. Because we'd hunted that place several times, we knew how the deer moved to escape from danger. We positioned ourselves in the bottleneck, and I took one of my best whitetails that day.

You can find bottlenecks with aerial photos and you can find them by physically scouting, before or after the season. Nothing beats sitting in a good stand and watching how deer move through the bottleneck.

9

Walking Silently

I learned a lot about deer hunting from a veteran named Clinton Berry. Mr. Berry was in my hunting club. He only hunted on weekends and he almost always got a buck. Everybody talked about how lucky he was, but Mr. Berry wasn't lucky, he was good. He preferred to still-hunt, and that's the toughest method for hunting whitetails. Mr. Berry showed me how to walk through the woods.

I was doing everything wrong until he showed me the secret, which is to move slowly, taking small steps. By small steps, I mean steps no larger than your foot size. I wear size

12, so I get to step farther than most folks, but that's still a small step. Another tip is to walk on the balls of your feet, not on your heels. When you take a long stride and put your foot down on your heel, you've already committed your weight. If you step on a stick, it breaks.

Some hunters walk as if they're trying to get their daily exercise, with their heads down to watch what they're stepping on. Mr. Berry taught me to walk with my head up. Keep your head down and you'll never see a deer before he sees you. Keep your head up, take small steps on the balls of your feet, and wear thin-soled boots when possible. That way, you can feel a limb or a twig as you step on it and stop before putting your entire weight down.

Mr. Berry put it this way: You have to feel like you're walking soft. You also have to move in slow motion and stay in the thick woods. Don't walk in the open woods. Move from one big tree to the next, using the trees as cover. Look around by moving your eyes. Don't jerk your head around and create unnecessary movement. Stay in the shadows and along edges.

Taking small, slow steps helps you maintain good balance and keeps your camo silhouette together. When you take long steps, you break up your camo. Knowing how to move quietly through the woods is important whether you're still-hunting, scouting, or heading for a stand.

Top photo shows hunter taking long strides—the wrong way to walk. Better to take small steps, as shown above.

10

Tracks
and Droppings

As simple as it sounds, every deer hunter should learn to recognize whitetail tracks and droppings. You really ought to learn to identify *all* the tracks you see in the woods, from turkeys to bears. It makes the time you spend in the woods much more interesting.

In much of the whitetail's range, deer share their habitat with livestock. A lot of the trails you see through the woods are livestock trails, not deer trails. Particularly when made by cows, these trails tend to be a lot more distinct, and I suspect that more than a few hunters waste their time setting up on cow trails. Learn what a deer track looks like, and look for those tracks.

A splayed hoofprint in a scrape is the telltale sign that a buck is using the area. *Credit: R. Thornberry*

You can't always tell a buck track from a doe track. I look for a pretty wide track with the hooves curled to the outside. If the track has a lot of depth to it and it's not spread out like the deer's been running, I'll bet that's a pretty big buck. If it's a doe, it might be the biggest doe in the world and I wouldn't mind shooting her where does are legal.

When you hunt deer in fresh snow, tracks are easier to read. Bucks tend to drag their feet more than does, and they particularly do so during the rut. If you've watched a buck chasing a doe, you know they run with a peculiar gait that you don't see at other times.

Lots of folks don't know what deer droppings look like, and you'd be surprised how many hunters go to the woods and mistake rabbit droppings for deer droppings. Both animals leave pellets, but rabbit droppings are round. Deer droppings are elongated and are sometimes misshapen. Fresh droppings are soft and easily mashed with the toe of a boot, while old droppings are more brittle and dry.

11

Finding Rubs

Bucks rub their antlers against brush and trees for two basic reasons. In late summer and early fall, the bucks are rubbing velvet off their antlers. This is not an aggressive rub, and you can sometimes find strands of velvet or a little blood on the brush. Bucks attempt to remove every piece of velvet from their hardened antlers, although non-typical bucks don't always get the job done.

Later in the fall, bucks are much more aggressive when creating antler rubs. Now they'll tear up the trees. They'll pick bigger trees, and you'll see shavings on the ground where they've really been grinding on the wood. Look

A buck making a rub on a large tree. Pay more attention to the height of scar marks left on a tree than the size of the tree itself, as it takes a big buck with a high rack to scar way up on a tree. *Credit: Ray Sasser*

at the ground, and you can often see that the buck really dug in to fight that tree.

Aggressive rubs serve two purposes. It's like a boxer working out on a heavy bag. Fighting a rub gets the buck's neck muscles into shape for combat with other bucks. A buck will also tear up a bush to display aggressively to a nearby rival. He's saying to the rival, "You want a piece of me?" or "Here's what's gonna happen to you if you don't back off!"

What a buck rub tells me is that there's a buck in the area. If several rubs are in a sequence, that's called a rub line. You can learn something about how bucks travel by studying rub lines. If all the rubs are on the same sides of the trees, you know which direction the bucks are coming from as they move through the area. If you find what looks like a fresh rub—the sap's still oozing, the ground is freshly disturbed— brush the shavings out of the way and smooth out the ground. Check the rub in a couple of days to see if the buck has come back.

I've seen some mighty big bucks tear up little bushes, but if I see a big tree that's torn up, I'll roll the dice and say that's a big deer. I'm more likely to pay attention to the height of scar marks left on a tree than the the size of the tree itself, as it takes a big buck with a high rack to scar way up on a tree.

12

Breeding Scrapes

Novice hunters often confuse the terms "scrape" and "rub." A scrape is a pawed-out area on the ground that's usually a foot to four feet in diameter. Scrapes almost invariably are located under an overhanging limb where a buck can hook the limb with his antlers and rub it with his face to leave scent from facial glands. He does this while urinating, with the urine running down his hocks and flushing his scent into the scrape. Then he paws the scrape and deposits scent from the glands in his hooves.

Simply stated, the scrape is a buck's notice in the personal ads that he's looking for romance. Estrus does come

Bucks usually start making scrapes about the same time every year, and they often make them in the same places. *Credit: R. Thornberry*

along, find the scrape, and deposit their own urine. A buck regularly checks his scrapes. When a doe has visited the scrape, the buck trails her and the ritual breeding chase begins.

A scrape is not just an indication that a buck is in the area. Rather, it means that not only has he been there, but chances are he'll come back. Some scrapes pay off better than others, probably because they're made in good locations. An active scrape really smells strong. You see a lot of leaves pawed away from the scrape. If you find four or five of these in a row, you've located what's known as a scrape line. Breeding scrapes are located in thicker areas, not in the wide open. They will usually have a lot of sign with them: droppings, fresh tracks, the smell of urine, and leaves kicked back around the scrape area. Find a breeding scrape, and you should consider putting up a stand to hunt.

Bucks usually start making breeding scrapes about the same time every year, and they often make them in the same places. Examine the scrape and see which direction the leaves have been pawed out. Compare that information to nearby trails and you have a good idea of how the bucks are approaching their scrapes.

The Buckmasters television crew and I filmed a scrape for five days in a row and saw all kinds of bucks coming to it. You can usually tell the dominant buck by how confidently he approaches. Subordinate bucks act nervous, because they know they're on dangerous ground. I like to hunt scrapes pre-rut and post-rut, when the bucks are most anxious to find does and are more likely to visit during daylight.

13

Looking For Deer In All The Wrong Places

To many deer hunters are looking for an animal much bigger than a deer. I call this tendency the "horse with antlers" mentality. Magazine photos and videos make whitetails seem much larger than they are. A mature buck stands about three feet to his back. The top of his rack is no higher than six feet off the ground. Everybody seems to think deer are going to be standing in the wide open, turned broadside with a bull's-eye painted on them. That won't hap-

When you're looking for deer, scan heavy cover. Look for a brown, horizontal line; a glint of an antler, nose, or eye; and movement. *Credit: Ray Sasser*

pen. The trick is being able to pick a deer out in the thickest cover.

When you're looking for a deer, start low on the forest floor and look no higher than three feet. I used to make the mistake of looking too high, and I probably looked over more deer than I saw. Particularly when still-hunting, hunters move through the woods with their eyes straight ahead, looking too high to see most deer. If a deer is bedded, its back is only a foot off the ground.

I'll never forget the first time I went still-hunting and saw a deer before it saw me. What I saw was a color that didn't fit with the woods. I looked and looked until the deer took shape and I recognized what it was. From that moment on, I knew a lot more about what I was looking for, and I got better at spotting deer.

I look for horizontal shapes and movement in the woods, but I also look for the deer's contrasting coloration— the white around the eyes and nose, the white throat patch, the white in the ears, the white inside the legs, the white on the tail, the black nose, the dark eyes, the black or dark hair on the end of the tail surrounded by white. These things stand out and are easier to notice.

14

Whitetail Body Language

Psychologists can interpret a person's mood by reading his body language, and a hunter can do the same thing with deer. Deer will give you a lot of signs, if you pay attention. I watch the deer's tail. If the tail gets in an arched position with the ears alert, something's wrong. When everything is all right, the deer will twitch its tail a few times and go back to feeding.

If a deer starts stomping its foot and tensing up, something's wrong. If the deer spots you in a stand and starts bobbing its head up and down, it's trying to get you to move and

Knowing what a deer is going to do can help you decide if and when to take a shot. In these photos, from upper left, the first deer is relaxed; the second is alarmed, and in full flight; and the third is aggressive (note the pinned-back ears—a sure sign). *Credit: George Barnett*

confirm its suspicions. When deer are staring at me and their body language is nervous, I'll sit absolutely still and even squint my eyes so less of the white shows in my eyeballs.

Pay special attention to the doe with a yearling. She's the spookiest animal in the woods. If I spook her, she will alert every other deer that's nearby. If mamma doe doesn't like whatever is happening, daddy isn't coming, either.

When you're watching deer in a field or other feeding situation, they'll tell you when other deer are coming. If the deer look up and stare into the cover, for example, that's a sign that another deer is approaching. If you're watching a little buck, he'll tip you off that a bigger buck is heading your way. Not only will a small buck watch a bigger buck approach; he'll act nervous. Deer have a fascinating way of communicating with one another through body language, and you'll pick it up if you watch carefully.

If the deer stamp and throw their flags up but don't immediately run off, there's probably a coyote or a bobcat coming. If deer smell a human, they don't wait around to see what's going to happen. If deer detect a four-legged predator, they'll make sure the other deer are alert, then they'll keep an eye on the danger until it moves away.

By studying whitetail body language, you learn to monitor the deer's level of anxiety and you can predict when they'll head for cover. And that's important in deciding when to take a shot.

15

Take A Stand

The most effective way to hunt white-tailed deer is to take a stand in a productive spot and just sit there quietly. Over the years, I've hunted whitetails in every kind of stand imaginable, from sunken blinds to high-rise towers. Mobile stands such as treestands and tripods (where there are no large trees) are practical because they allow you to adjust to deer movements.

Stands work for a number of reasons. We're playing a cat-and-mouse game with whitetails. Deer are using all their senses to detect danger and we're using our senses—mostly our sight—to locate game. What generally attracts your attention to a deer? Movement. Your eye is attracted to the move-

Hunting from the trees is one of the most effective ways to take a buck. These three stands are all up high, with adequate brush to break up the hunters' silhouettes. *Credit: R. Thornberry*

ment. When you're moving through the woods, it's the movement that the deer sees. If you sit perfectly still, a deer can look right at you and not recognize the danger.

In this predator-prey game we're playing, whichever side is moving is at a disadvantage. That's one reason sitting still is so effective. When you hunt from an elevated stand, which I prefer, you're also getting your scent above the deer. I use API climbing stands, fixed-position stands with ladder sticks, and ladder stands. Just don't get the idea that being 20 feet up a tree makes you invisible. Deer *will* look up and they *will* see you in a treestand. Air currents will move your scent down to the deer, particularly in the afternoon when the temperature is cooling and the air currents are moving downhill. In the mornings, your scent generally rises.

There's no such thing as a perfect stand for all locations. In thick woods, you may have to sit on the ground because the canopy blocks your vision when you're up in a tree. If you're afraid of heights, you can still be very successful hunting from a ground stand, but you have to be completely aware of the wind direction. You should also cut some brush to break up your outline and find a good tree to lean against so you can be as comfortable as possible. The idea is to sit still for long periods of time. Even the best stand won't work if it's located in a poor site.

16

Treestand Strategy

I do a lot of hunting from treestands, particularly in the South. When you set up the stand, play the prevailing winds but also pay attention to the sun. If it's a morning stand, you don't want the stand to face the rising sun. It may be possible to set up on a trail or food source so you're never looking into the sun—morning or afternoon. Some stand locations work best in the morning and others are better in the afternoon.

I'm always looking for what I call the perfect tree, but it doesn't exist in every situation. I've gone so far as to install a 40-foot utility pole in a place I wanted to hunt and hang a treestand from it. That setup works great if the pole has trees

Big bucks call for drastic measures—in this case, a utility pole placed between cover-providing trees. *Credit: Aduston Rogers*

around it to break up your outline. If I'm hunting a treestand in a slick tree, I'll brush up the stand with limbs cut from nearby trees. Even when you're 20 feet high, you still have to hide from the deer.

Two pieces of equipment I recommend for treestand hunters are a telescoping limb saw and a racheting hand pruner. The saw lets you cut shooting lanes, and the pruner is used for trimming leafy limbs that will make noise if you brush up against them. When you set up a stand, hopefully before the season, check out all your shooting angles and do your pruning during the setup. If you leave stands in place from one season to the next, don't forget to get in the woods early to adjust the stands to compensate for tree growth during the year and also to trim obstacles that have grown up in your shooting lanes. When leaving stands in trees after the season, loosen the straps or chains. This gives the tree a chance to grow without binding your stand.

When I approach a treestand, I try to stay away from the trails I think deer will be using. The first chance is the best chance when you're hunting mature bucks. If the wind changes to an unfavorable direction while I'm hunting, I'll bail out of that stand rather than risk spooking a good deer.

17

Spot and Stalk

One of my favorite ways to hunt deer in open country is to use a technique called spot and stalk. It means locating a buck in the distance, then using the terrain to slip in close enough for a shot. I often use this technique to hunt the canyon country out West, but it works anywhere you've got good visibility and elevation.

In addition to my 10-power binoculars, I carry a 16-47× Nikon spotting scope and a portable tripod in my backpack. If I see a deer at half a mile or more, I set up the spotting scope to try and determine whether it's a buck I want to go after. I can't tell you how many hours I've spent stalking bucks that were too far to evaluate with binoculars and then passed up the shot because the bucks weren't big enough. The spotting scope saves me a lot of steps.

Whenever you're hunting in open country, stay off the skyline and try to keep the sun at your back. That makes it harder for game to spot you. Once I see a buck that I want, I then study the terrain and figure out how to get close enough for the shot without the deer seeing or smelling me. Sometimes, that means crawling for long distances. Other times, you can get behind some brush or get down under a hill where the deer can't see you. When I get under a hill or behind some cover, I'll hustle to close the distance.

If you can see the deer, he can see you. You don't want to move if he's looking in your direction, because it's the movement he's most likely to see. I move when the deer puts his head down to feed or looks in the other direction. Spot and stalk is an exciting way to hunt because you know the deer is there, and it's a real challenge to sneak within shooting distance.

In open country, good binoculars are a huge help in spotting deer at a distance. A spotting scope can then help you determine if the deer is worth stalking.

18

The Rut

One thing every deer hunter should know is the approximate time of the whitetail breeding season in the area he hunts. Spend as much time in the woods as possible during the rut. Whitetail breeding seasons vary tremendously around the country. Some ruts begin as early as September and others run through January. State biologists can tell you the rutting schedule for your area.

The rut is critical because this is the time of the season when a mature buck is most likely to move during daylight hours. The buck's instinct to breed is so strong that he'll throw caution to the wind as he travels to find estrus does. I've taken a lot of good bucks during the rut, and I try to schedule my hunts to coincide with the rut whenever possible.

A big buck checks out a doe, to see if she's receptive, while a submissive buck looks on. *Credit: Ray Sasser*

Learn to recognize rutting behavior. If you see a buck trailing with his nose to the ground like a bird dog, you can bet he's following a doe. He usually doesn't get to breed the doe as soon as he finds her, either. Unless the timing is perfect, the doe leads the buck on a chase that's designed to attract the attention of other dominant bucks. In country where there are a lot of bucks, it's not unusual to see several bucks chasing one doe. The dominant buck will breed and pass on his superior genes, but he may have to fight off his rivals before he does so.

If you see a buck with a doe during the rut, chances are good he won't leave that doe. If the doe comes across an opening, get ready. The buck will be close behind. It's also helpful to know that breeding chases often follow an unpredictable route and may circle back repeatedly. If a chase comes by your stand and you don't get a shot, stay ready in case the deer come back.

It's also possible to see a breeding chase in the distance and hustle to get within range. The deer are so involved in the breeding ritual that they're less wary than usual. Bucks only have a couple of weeks a year to breed. Think about it— they've been wary the whole year, until now. If it worked that way with people, I'd be the first buck shot every year.

When hunting during the rut, get ready if you see a doe running low to the ground in a permissive way. A buck is on her tail. Another tip is to listen for buck grunts. Bucks often grunt when they're on the trail of a hot doe. Be ready, because the buck will be on the move.

In The Stand

Reflections
On The Hunt

Jackie Bushman and son Jackie, with a Thanksgiving buck in Alabama. This is what deer hunting is all about.

The object of our desires. Will he stand
still, and give you a shot?

. . . or will he notice something is not quite right, and
move out of range, leaving you with only a memory?

Two big bucks square off in a pre-rut battle. Hunters who use rattling antlers at this stage of the rut have an excellent chance of calling in a buck, especially in areas with good buck to doe ratios. *Credit: VA Dept. of Game and Inland Fisheries*

Though seemingly at ease, these two bucks will battle at a second's notice if an estrus doe comes by. *Credit: VA Dept. of Game and Inland Fisheries*

The smart hunter is the hunter who scouts before the season. Here, the author inspects an aerial photograph of an area he intends to hunt.

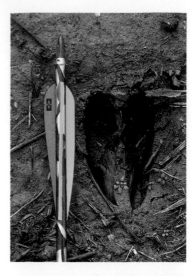

Large, deeply imbedded hoofprints mean a big deer, possibly a trophy buck. *Credit: R. Thornberry*

Find concentrations of acorns such as these, and you've found an area where deer will eventually feed. These are white oak acorns, whitetail favorites. *Credit: R. Thornberry*

Heavily traveled, generational trails are always good bets for hunting. Set your stand back far enough so you aren't easily detected by deer moving along the trail. Notice which direction the tracks are going. They will give you clues as to where to place your stand and when to hunt it. *Credit: R. Thornberry*

Glassing with binoculars is a must in open country; it not only lets you find deer, but helps you evaluate them as well. A spotting scope helps you zero in and really inspect deer before you begin stalking.

Once you have found an area you want to hunt, it's time to get serious. Good boots are critical.

Getting an edge: For bowhunters, practice clearly makes a difference. Maintain proper form until your arrow hits its intended target.

Scent eliminators and deer attractants can truly give you an advantage if you use them properly.

Another edge is staying warm. Overboots keep feet warm, no matter how far the temperature may drop. *Credit: R. Thornberry*

The author with an Idaho buck he took on a silent drive. When bucks are in thick cover, drives may be the only way to get them out.

Glassing thick cover, where big bucks go when the pressure is on.

How many big bucks will you take in your lifetime? They don't happen every day, but when they do, you'd better be ready with a good
camera and plenty of film. Set up the shot, shoot a few rolls of film,
from all angles; you'll only get one chance for photos of a buck such
as this before he's off to the taxidermist. *Credit: Ray Sasser*

A monster buck in cover. When hunting, look for 'parts' of deer, not the whole animal. Horizontal lines, glinting antlers or eyes, flicking ears—all such signs merit closer investigation. *Credit: Ray Sasser*

The author on the trail. Rub lines (note rub at right) can tell you not only that bucks are present, but the direction in which they are travelling.

Two nice bucks tending a doe. If you stalked to within range of these two, which one would you take? (Hint—check out the drop tine on the deer on the left.) *Credit: Ray Sasser*

Bucks make many scrapes in the pre-rut—it's the ones they freshen a few weeks later, in thick areas, that you should pay particular attention to. *Credit: Ray Sasser*

Use a safety belt, always; place your stand overlooking a well-used trail or buck core area; make sure you're in a tree backgrounded by other trees, to break up your silhouette, as deer do look up; and you've placed the odds in your favor. *Credit: R. Thornberry*

A big-bodied Texas buck doing what rutting bucks often do; being unpredictable by being out in the open in the middle of the day. If you haven't filled your tag, it may make sense to stay out all day. *Credit: George Barnett*

No matter what type of hunting you do—still-hunting, stand hunting, stalking, rattling, calling—always watch the wind. The big bucks do. *Credit: Ray Sasser*

Buck battles: They're violent, they're not fooling around, and some deer become seriously injured in the process. *Credit: George Barnett*

Author inspecting sheds, post-season. Finding such antlers can help you plan your next season's hunting strategy.

The author takes careful aim with his rifle. Quality optics make all the difference—not only in low-light conditions, but in daylight as well.

A monster bucks grunts at a distant, estrus doe. Hunters using grunt calls can often draw bucks into range during the rut. *Credit: Ray Sasser*

Drawing a bead with bow and arrow. Take your time, keep your form, and never shoot at ranges beyond what you feel comfortable with—no matter how big the buck!

The author approaches a good-sized buck he took with a shotgun in Lowndes County, Alabama. A shotgun can be effective out to 100 yards, especially if you have a good scope and a solid rest.

Bushman and outfitter Tim Craig take a bearing before heading off into the Idaho mountains. Many people think of whitetails as eastern and southern deer, but western states also have huge herds.

The author used a bipod to get a rest before taking this Idaho buck with one well-placed shot to the heart/lung region.

Treat every deer as if it's still alive, until you're certain it's not. If his eyes are closed, get ready for a second shot. Always approach from the rear.

Big bucks are more active early and late in the day, when the light is low. The only major exception is during the rut, when the bucks throw caution to the wind and start chasing estrus does. *Credit: Ray Sasser*

19

Use the
Grunt Stop

I don't like to shoot at a deer that's moving. Your odds of making a good shot are much better when the deer is standing perfectly still. There are lots of different sounds you can make to stop a deer for a shot. Some hunters whistle while others might yell. I've yelled at a buck or two myself, but only when they were at long range and usually when they were running or moving fast. Deer have phenomenal hearing, but they don't hear as well when they're moving because the sounds they're making mask the sounds around them.

I prefer not to whistle or yell at a buck. The deer might stop on a whistle or the sound of a human voice, but that's not a sound he's accustomed to hearing and he'll be alert to possible danger. If you whistle or yell to stop a deer, he might stop to locate the sound, then take off even faster. I prefer making a grunting sound with my voice, like a gutteral *eh* that imitates a buck grunt. That's a sound that deer are used to hearing. A buck that hears another buck grunting will stop to pinpoint the deer's location but he won't be particularly alarmed. During certain times of the season when I might use a grunt call, I'll take the small insert out of the Woods Wise buck and doe call and use it as a grunt stop.

One mistake you can make with the grunt stop is not being prepared for the shot. I want my crosshairs or my bowsight on the deer when I grunt. When bowhunting, I'm at full draw and ready to release the arrow. The deer may not stand still for long and you've got to be ready to make the shot as soon as he stops. I frequently use the grunt stop when deer are moving through heavy cover where a limb might deflect a bullet or an arrow. I wait until the deer gets to an open lane and then grunt. I make the shot as soon as the deer stops in the opening.

When a deer is moving through cover, grunting can sometimes make him stop long enough for you to take a shot. Just make sure you have a clear shooting lane before sounding off. *Credit: Ray Sasser*

20

Antler Rattling

Rattling up bucks is one of the most talked-about hunting methods we have. In most places where whitetails are hunted, rattling doesn't work very well because does greatly outnumber bucks and there aren't many mature bucks. Rattling works best in a well-balanced deer herd where the buck-to-doe ratio is pretty close.

That's the situation where bucks are most likely to fight. They fight over breeding rights to individual does and also over territory. When well-matched, mature bucks get into a fight, it can be brutal. Most buck fights don't last long before the weaker deer is overmatched, but well-matched bucks may fight for hours, rest between rounds, then go at it again.

Rattling works best in areas that have relatively even buck to doe ratios. When setting up, pay special attention to the area downwind of your position, as that's where wary bucks like to approach from.

Shed antlers or average buck antlers that you don't want to mount make good rattling horns. I like to use antlers from the same side of the rack—two right-side antlers, for instance—as I'm less likely to gore myself when the antlers curve the same way. Use a grinder to remove the brow tines and smooth the burrs off the antler bases. Drill a hole in the bases so you can fit them with a carrying string or leather thong.

When rattling, I always start slow, just grinding the antlers or tickling the tines together to make sounds that are recognizable but won't startle any buck that may be close by. Fighting whitetails don't run together like mountain sheep do. Rather, they lock antlers and get in a shoving match. There's more grinding than clashing. To make the "fight" sound realistic, you should slash the brush, rub the antlers against trees, thump the ground, roll rocks—you can't make too much noise once you get started. You can also mix in grunts while rattling.

Rattling works best if you have one hunter handling the antlers and the other hunter doing the shooting. Bucks may come within seconds of hearing the first sounds, and while they may come running directly to the sounds, they're more likely to circle and try to get downwind of the fight. There's an art to setting up for deer rattling. You should try to keep an open area downwind. Hunters never see the majority of bucks they rattle up. The bucks come in cautiously, circle downwind, figure the deal out, then slip away without being seen. When rattling works, it's one of the most exciting ways to hunt whitetails.

21

Nose of
The Whitetail

Deer have an incredible sense of smell. I've even seen them react to the scent of wood shavings, where we had sawed a limb to open a shooting lane. When I'm hunting with a cameraman, the human smell is doubled and I have to do everything possible to defeat a wary buck's nose. There's no substitute for paying attention to the wind and staying downwind of where you expect to see a deer.

Since deer and weather do unpredictable things, I rely on cover scents to help mask my odor. That's especially important when you're bowhunting and the deer has to be close

A big buck curls his lip, testing the air for scent. *Credit: Ray Sasser*

in order to get a shot. I use fox urine sometimes, but I mostly use raccoon scent, as raccoons are common just about everywhere in the country. Since I usually hunt from treestands and raccoons spend a lot of time in trees, I use a spray bottle of Tink's Bandit Coon Scent and put it all around us in the tree. If you're putting out cover scent on the ground, always put it downwind of the stand. On a still day, put it all around the stand because your human scent radiates in a circle when there's no wind.

When it gets close to the rut, I put out Tink's Trophy Buck Urine, both as a cover scent and as an attractor. I'll put tarsal glands around a scrape I'm hunting and, when the timing is right, I'll use Tink's 69 Doe In Rut Buck Lure. In states where the bag limit is liberal, you can take the tarsal glands from a harvested buck and use them. You can also remove the urine from a harvested buck or doe's bladder and know you've got the freshest product available.

If you visit a locker plant or a state check station on opening day, you can usually get plenty of tarsal glands. They smell strong, and a lot of hunters will be glad to have you remove the glands for them so they don't get the smell on themselves and so the glands don't contaminate the venison. I like to use tarsal glands, especially when I'm antler rattling, because they're as natural as you can possibly get.

22

People Stink

Cover scents are valuable for masking human odor, but you can further your cause by eliminating as many foreign smells as possible. I shower with unscented soap and I use unscented deodorant. I spray my outer clothes and boots with an odor neutralizer. I brush my teeth before heading for the stand, whether it's morning or midday, because I'm convinced that a deer can smell my breath.

I know there are hunters who smoke in their stands and dip smokeless tobacco, and they sometimes take the biggest buck in the woods. Anything can happen if the deer is upwind, but it just makes good sense to eliminate all the odors that might alarm a whitetail.

Anything you can do to mask or neutralize your human scent will help improve your odds for success. I wash my clothes in scent-free soap and then put them into a Scent-Lok bag to prevent them from picking up odors before the hunt.

One of the best products I've found for combatting human scent is the Scent-Lok clothing system. Scent-Lok uses a filtered charcoal technology to absorb the human scent. Even if you're 15 feet up a tree, when you've got two people, including a cameraman, chances are the deer will smell you when they get downwind. When Gene Bidlespacher (Buckmasters cameraman) and I started using Scent-Lok suits, our success rate went up significantly. My Scent-Lok suit has a hood, and that hood is a key element, because a lot of your human scent comes from your head. I pull my Scent-Lok hood up over my nose and it doubles as a face mask.

I use a Scent-Lok suit as an extra layer of underwear. I've also got a Scent-Lok bag that I keep all my hunting clothes in. I don't get dressed at the camp and I don't wear my hunting clothes in the truck. I keep a mat in the hunting vehicle and I lay the mat out on the ground when I get to where we're going to hunt. Then I get my hunting clothes out of the Scent-Lok bag and put them on. When I leave the field, I take off my hunting clothes and boots and put them back in the Scent-Lok bag, organizing them in the order I'll put them on next time. It's a lot of trouble, but it keeps foreign odors from permeating my clothes, and it works.

23

Silent Drives

There are times when the deer are simply not moving and you're forced to make something happen. Maybe you're up against a full moon or hot weather conditions. I like to use a silent drive to force deer to move.

By silent drive, you're not using dogs to make the deer move and you're not moving through cover, yelling and making a commotion to scare the deer. When deer are panicked, they're liable to bust out of the cover on a dead run, and any shot you get will be tough to make.

A silent drive is different. It means playing the wind to carry the driver's scent into a bedding area. That makes the deer concerned enough to sneak away from danger but not

Silent drives work especially well in woodlot habitat such as this. *Credit: R. Thornberry*

panicked enough to run. When you're setting up a silent drive, it's important to know the lay of the land and how deer move from one patch of cover to the next. An aerial photo is very useful for finding bottlenecks that deer travel as escape corridors, but there's no substitute for having an intimate knowledge of the place you're hunting and for having watched deer move through there in the past. On a silent drive, I try to think like a deer and determine how the deer will react to a threat.

Silent drives work very well in woodlot habitat where deer are likely to move from one patch of cover to the next. In many smaller woodlots, you may not have to penetrate the cover. Just the human smell moving downwind from the edge of the cover may cause deer to move out. Driving deer in big stands of dense woods is tougher because the deer have a lot more escape options and it's harder to predict which way they'll go.

Safety is the primary concern on any deer drive. The hunters should wear hunter orange, even if the law doesn't require it. Everyone should also know everyone else's whereabouts.

24

Clothes Make
The Deer Hunter

I get cold quickly, so it's important for me to dress warmly. If you're not warm, you can't sit still and concentrate on what you're doing and you may as well go home. Some people make fun of all the clothes I wear, but I've been cold too many times, and I've worked out a system that allows me to hunt in the brutal cold. One key is to buy clothing in sizes bigger than you ordinarily wear so it can be comfortably layered.

Some of the stuff I wear may not look too cool, but I'm not dressing for a fashion show. I'd rather dress for warmth than for looks. I wear finger Whitewater mittens for gloves.

Dressing in layers will help you stay warm and keep your scent under control. Shown here taking a break from taping a show, the author also wears rubber boots for extra scent control. *Credit: R. Thornberry*

You can wear them as a complete mitten or you can fold the end of the mitten back to leave your fingers exposed. When I take a shot, whether it's with a bow, rifle, or shotgun, I want to touch my trigger or my release with the skin of my hand.

I dress in layers that may include more than one set of thermal underwear, and always includes a Scent-Lok suit (see Tip 22, People Stink). In extremely cold weather, for example, I wear three pairs of thermal underwear. One pair is large, the next is X-large, and the third is XX-large. My jacket size will be XX-large so I can get extra clothes on. My pants will be a 38 waist when they are normally 36. You do this to avoid binding your arms and legs. The outer layer will be Liberty or Dux-Bak 6-pocket pants or bib overalls in the Realtree camo pattern at least a size larger than my other clothes.

For boots, I wear rubber-soled boots made by La-Crosse with different insulation value, depending on how cold the weather is. The rubber-soled boots seem to work well for me because they don't leave as much scent where I walk and they're ideal for hunting in snow or wading in water. The main thing is to wear clothes that are comfortable and will allow you to sit still in any kind of weather. It's better to have too many clothes than not enough. You can always take off a layer if you get hot.

25

Gizmos

Chemical heat packs are a great invention for cold-weather hunters. When I'm hunting in bitter cold, I've got heat packs stuck everywhere. They generate heat through a chemical reaction, and they make a real difference.

One item I like to wear around my waist is a muff-style handwarmer by Whitewater. It has zippered pockets for my knife and other accessories, and I also keep a heat pack in there so I can warm up my hands. When I open up my mittens to expose my fingers, I put a heat pack into the pouch that covers my fingers.

I also wear a kidney belt with heat packs against my kidneys, and they really help me stay warm. When I used to play professional tennis in the South, I'd often compete non-

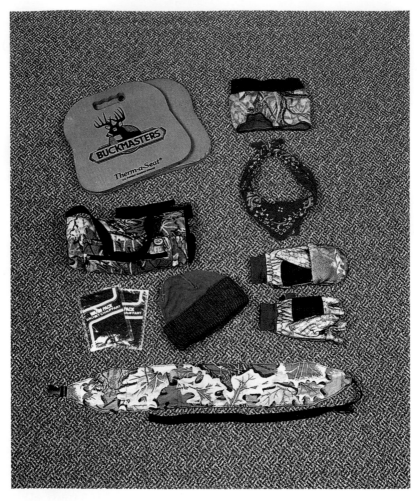

Some of the ancillary gear that the author likes to carry afield includes chemical heat packs, hard warmer, toboggan, and Therm-a-Seats.

stop for four hours, and sometimes more, in temperatures as high as 100°F with a heat index of 140°F. To stay cool I used to take ice and wrap it in a bandana, then wrap it around my neck.

When it's cold, I wrap a heat pack in a bandana and wrap that around my neck. I've got a long neck and I lose body heat if it's exposed, so I wear a bandana with a heat pack, a turtleneck shirt, and a skiing dickey. The heat pack also helps keep my neck from getting stiff so I can turn my head and keep a sharp watch for deer. I learned a long time ago that I can't expose my skin, particularly my neck, to severe cold and sit still for eight hours.

For headgear in cold weather, I wear a reversible toboggan by Whitewater. It's camo on one side and fluorescent orange on the other. In Alabama, you don't have to wear hunter orange once you've climbed above 12 feet, so I start up the tree with the orange side out, then reverse it when I reach the top.

I also carry two Therm-a-Seats—padded cushions that keep me from sitting on a cold, hard metal or plastic stand, the cold ground, or a rock. I also put a Therm-a-Seat on the platform of my treestand. This keeps my feet warm where the cold metal stand can't suck the warmth out of my boots. If you don't have a Therm-a-Seat, put some camo fleece down. It will keep your feet warm and the noise down. In brutally cold weather, I use boot blankets over my boots.

26

Backpacks

I take a backpack wherever I hunt. It's a great device for organizing gear. If you'll keep all your essential equipment in your backpack, you'll know where it is all the time and you won't be scrambling at the last minute trying to find something.

A rainsuit is just one item that always goes into my backpack. So does a saw, flashlight, toilet paper, extra cartridges, snacks, water, cover scents, attractant scents, first aid kit, seat cushions, matches—you name it. Whatever you think you might need on a deer hunt should go into your backpack. If you're hunting in unfamiliar country, throw in an aerial photo, a topo map, or a GPS unit. A hand-held radio can be a

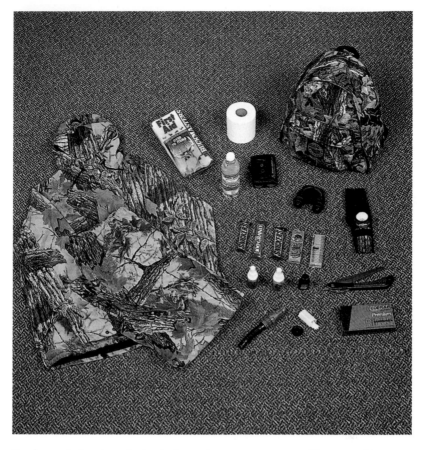

Bushman's backpack includes raingear, scents, calls, portable saw, first-aid kit, flashlight, and other necessities.

useful safety accessory, too. If you have a problem, use the radio to call a buddy. If you get hot during the hunting day, shed clothes and stuff them in the backpack.

I frequently use my backpack as a shooting rest. In fact, I was leaning against a fencepost with my backpack in my lap, using it for a rest, when I shot the biggest buck of my life. That was in Alberta. I've used it the same way in a treestand, too. If you have to make a long shot over open ground, a backpack makes a great rest from a prone position. When I'm shooting from the ground off a bipod, my backpack becomes an elbow rest.

A backpack used for whitetail hunting should be made from one of the newer fleece materials that don't make a lot of noise when you brush up against a limb while walking through the woods. It pays to be as quiet as you can, even when you're just heading to a stand location. You never know when a big buck might hear some noise he doesn't like and decide to go the other way. I use a backpack made by Whitewater. It has a Scent-Lok lining.

27

Ammunition

You should shoot a variety of ammunition in your rifle or shotgun to see which works best in your particular gun. Once you decide on a bullet design and brand that suits your style of hunting, make sure you sight in with the same brand, bullet design, and bullet weight that you'll use when hunting. Changing any of those three variables can cause a slight shift in where your gun shoots.

I shoot Federal Premium ammunition, which costs more than standard bullets but is loaded to very fine tolerances. In fact, premium ammo is the next best thing to handloading your own ammunition, which I don't have the time or the inclination to do. Several companies now make premium ammunition, and it's worth the added cost. Ammunition cost

When deciding on a cartridge, experiment with several brands, designs, and weights until you come upon that one that works best in your rifle. *Credit: Ray Sasser*

is a small part of deer hunting and most hunters shoot fewer than two boxes of cartridges a year. That includes sighting in, practice rounds, and hunting.

A tip that's particularly important for hunters who travel from the city to hunt in rural areas is to make sure you have at least two boxes of cartridges with you. You never know when your rifle might take a lick that knocks it out of sync, and it may take several shots to get the rifle back to shooting where you want it. If you're hunting out in the boon-docks, the local hardware store might not carry your favorite brand of ammunition. That's especially true if you shoot premium loads or an unusual caliber or bullet design.

Some hunters prefer a fast, light bullet and others like a heavy bullet that's moving a little slower. They will all take deer. For hunting mature bucks, deer heavier than 200 pounds, I'd recommend 130-grain or heavier bullets. As long as you stick with a well-designed bullet and concentrate on making a good first shot, you won't have many problems.

28

Ballistics

I like to study ballistics charts because they help me fully understand what my ammunition will do at long range. The Federal Cartridge Company publishes a ballistics chart in its catalog, and ballistics charts are also available on the Internet and through most good gun stores.

The Federal chart shows bullet drop out to 500 yards, and how the bullet drifts in a crosswind. This will really help you, especially if you're used to hunting where shots are close and you're planning a deer hunting trip to wide-open spaces where long shots are more likely. Modern rifles and bullets will do their job at very long distances, but only if you know where to hold so the bullet hits its target.

CLASSIC CENTERFIRE RIFLE BALLISTICS

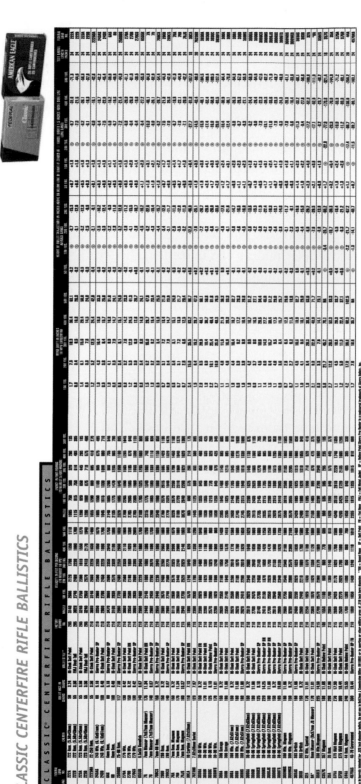

Ballistics charts will help you determine the type of bullet design and weight that work best for you.

Studying a ballistics chart will also help you in selecting the bullet design and weight to shoot in your rifle. It can likewise help you determine what caliber will work best for your style of whitetail hunting. For instance, the .35 Remington, a popular caliber for deer hunters in the thick woods of the East and South, works fine in close quarters. If you have to make a 400-yard shot with a .35-caliber rifle sighted to be dead on at 200 yards, you'd have to hold 70 inches above the target! Few deer hunters can make that shot work.

A 7mm Magnum sighted dead-on at 200 yards only drops about 20 inches at 400 yards, and that's a doable deal for a good rifle shot with a solid rest. I like to study the ballistics table like it's homework and I'm getting ready for a pop test. If you have trouble remembering numbers, write your particular ballistics on white adhesive tape and tape it to the inside of your rear scope cover or laminate the numbers in plastic and tape them to your rifle stock. You can even keep a laminated ballistics card handy in an outside pocket of your backpack. If the deer is that far away, you'll probably have enough time to find your ballistics cheat sheet.

29

Binoculars

Every deer hunter needs binoculars. I use small, compact Nikons for bowhunting and, I've got a pair of Nikon 10×40s for use in open country. It makes me nervous every time I hear a deer hunter say he doesn't need binoculars because he has a scope on his rifle.

Binoculars will help you see and evaluate deer, whether you hunt in the wide open spaces of the West or the thick woods of the South. In dense cover, binoculars gather light on a cloudy day or during the low-light witching hours of dawn and dusk when big bucks are most likely to move. You can look at a thicket with binoculars and pick out an ear or a throat patch that you could not see with your naked eye.

Whether you hunt open country in the West or dense woods in the South and East, good-quality binoculars can be invaluable. *Credit: R. Thornberry*

In open country, I've glassed bucks at hundreds of yards and determined whether they were potential "shooters" or not. Binoculars will help you study bucks a long way off, and they'll help you find bucks that are closer than you think.

Binoculars can also cost you deer. By that, I mean still-hunters in thick cover have an average of four seconds to get on the deer before he spooks. If you spend that brief time looking the buck over with binoculars, you won't have time enough to get your gun up. When you see a deer in close cover, you need to evaluate that deer through your scope. If you decide to take the deer, all you have to do is flip the safety off.

You should try out several different styles of binoculars at your sporting-goods store to see which focus systems and which eye relief works best for you. All binoculars look good in bright light. Go to the store at dusk and ask a salesman to step outside with you to test the binoculars in low light. Look at license plates on cars in the distance to see which binoculars are the sharpest and the brightest.

30

Rangefinders

One of the greatest technological inventions to come around in recent years is the laser rangefinder. When hunters miss a long shot, whether it's across a beanfield in Mississippi, across a wheat field in Kansas, on the other side of a Montana canyon, or down a South Texas sendero, 90 percent of the misses go high. That's because they overestimate the range and hold over the deer, thinking they're shooting 500 yards when they're only shooting 300.

A laser rangefinder—Nikon makes a Buckmaster 800 that works out to 800 yards—takes the guesswork out of distances, whether you're shooting 30 yards with a bow or 330 yards with a rifle. When I sit down in a bow stand, the first thing I do is take out my rangefinder and check the distances

Rangefinders help take the guesswork out of distances—you KNOW if you're shooting at 20 or 30 yards with a bow, or 150 or 200 with a rifle. *Credit: Ray Sasser*

to various trees and bushes all around the stand—wherever I might get a shot at a deer. My effective range for bowhunting is 30 yards, and I'll use the rangefinder to determine 30-yard landmarks all around the stand. When a buck comes inside those landmarks, the game has just started. If he stays outside the magic circle, he wins.

If you don't have a rangefinder, you can measure distances with your eyes. Look at a leaf on the ground right under your stand, then find a leaf about one yard out, then go to the next leaf and eventually figure out your maximum range. I used to do it that way before I had a laser rangefinder. Of course, you can also pace off distances to various landmarks, but the best time to do that is before hunting season. You can put orange tape around trees at those distances, or use different colors for different yardages.

The rangefinder is an educational tool. After I used one on dozens of deer and saw how far they really were, I got pretty good at judging the range. Before I used these devices, I was just as apt as anyone else to misjudge distances. Most deer hunters hunt in areas where the average shot is less than 100 yards. When they get in open country and the biggest deer they've ever seen is standing 250 or 300 yards away, they're lost—unless, of course, they have a rangefinder.

31

Scope It Out

I'm a firm believer in using scope sights wherever they're legal. I use a scope on my rifle, my muzzleloader, and my shotgun. Some states don't allow scopes during primitive weapons seasons, so be sure and check regulations before hunting with a scope.

Many deer hunters think they don't need a scope because they hunt in thick cover and the shots are pretty close. The magnification of a scope helps when you're making long shots, but it can also make a difference on close shots. What the scope does is focus your aiming point to a very precise spot on that deer. You don't just shoot at the deer: You shoot at a specific spot on the deer.

Scopes not only help you with long-range shots, but with closer distances as well. *Credit: Joe Songer*

Even at close range, the scope gathers light when the deer are most likely to be active, and it allows you to detect tiny obstructions such as limbs that might deflect the bullet. If you do all your hunting in the woods and never take a long shot, use a low-power scope, something such as a 4×. If you're like most deer hunters and you hunt in different places, from thick woods to open fields, I'd recommend a variable scope.

I use Nikon scopes, and my favorite model is a 3-9× variable with a 50mm objective lens. The big objective lens gathers more light in low-light situations. At low magnification, the scope works well for hunting in thick woods.

I can crank it up to $9\times$ and feel confident about making a long shot.

One tip for using a variable scope is to always leave it set on the lowest power. That gives you the widest field of view and allows you to quickly find a deer that appears close to your stand or suddenly jumps up while you're still-hunting. If you see a deer in the distance, you'll probably have time to change the scope to a higher power setting. At close range, you won't have time to adjust.

32

Guns and Bows

There's no simple answer as to what kind of gun or bow you should use for deer hunting. You should hunt with whatever you feel comfortable with, so long as it works on the deer in your area.

With rifles, there are lots of variables to consider when you're choosing calibers—the two most obvious being the size of the deer you hunt and the range of the average shot. I generally shoot a Remington Model 700 bolt action in 7mm Magnum, and it works great everywhere I hunt whitetails. I sometimes shoot a .270, which is a classic whitetail caliber.

The bolt-action style of rifle is inherently more accurate than the pump or autoloader. Deer hunters in thick woods sometimes favor these latter actions because they can deliver

Which rifle (or shotgun or bow) is for you? There is no pat answer:
Much depends on what you feel comfortable with. *Credit: Ray Sasser*

quick second shots, but my theory is to make the first shot a
good one and then you don't have to worry about a follow-up.
I load backup cartridges in the magazine of my bolt action, but
I approach each shot as if I only have one bullet.

Choosing a shotgun or muzzleloader that you can
shoot accurately is critical, but remember that both types of
firearms have limited ranges that you should not try to exceed.
I hunt with a Remington Premier 12-gauge autoloading slug
shotgun and a .50 caliber Knight muzzleloader. Shooting Federal sabots, the shotgun is plenty accurate. And except for the
slow reloading time and the smoke discharge when you shoot,
the muzzleloader is like shooting a centerfire rifle. The thing

to remember about a muzzleloader is that it's a fraction of a second slower to fire than a centerfire rifle. With a muzzleloader, you have to hang in there with the follow-through after you squeeze the trigger.

I shoot a Jennings compound bow with a mechanical release and a Keller pendulum sight. That's what I feel comfortable with, and it works for me. If you enjoy hunting with a wooden longbow and homemade arrows, that's great. Just be certain that you understand its limitations—and the limitations of whatever equipment you use—and don't try to exceed them.

33

Sighting In

It is absolutely necessary to sight in your deer rifle before you go hunting. You owe it to the deer to make certain your rifle shoots where you point it. Even if you just bought a rifle and the sporting-goods store bore-sighted the gun with a collimator, you still need to shoot it and fine-tune the point of impact. Bore sighting can be very precise, and can make the rifle shoot close enough to hit a paper target at 25 yards, but it's not meant to be a substitute for sighting in the rifle on a range.

Twenty five yards is where you should start shooting when you take a new rifle to the range. You can hire somebody to sight the rifle in for you, but I don't recommend that. You need to know how to make adjustments to your sights, no matter if you shoot a scope or open sights. If your sights get

It's critical to sight in your rifle to be as accurate as possible. Start at closer ranges, such as 25 yards, then work out to longer and longer distances, depending upon the types of ranges you expect to encounter when hunting. *Credit: Ray Sasser*

knocked off while you're hunting, you'll have to resight the rifle yourself and you need to know how it works. Besides, the more you shoot your rifle at targets, the more likely you are to make an accurate shot on a deer.

Take your rifle to a range where you've got a solid bench to shoot from and sandbags to create a solid rifle rest. You want that rifle rock solid, which will help you be as accurate as possible. For safety, always wear hearing protection and shooting glasses on the range.

Most popular deer rifles that are shooting slightly low at 25 yards will be about two inches high at 100 yards. Hunters who take shots at 200 to 300 yards usually sight in a little high at 100 yards. If you never take a shot beyond 100 yards, sight in to be dead on at that distance.

Anytime you've put a rifle on an airplane, you should shoot it at a target before you hunt, just to make sure it's still sighted in correctly. For that matter, you should fire at a target every now and then throughout the hunting season. Once they're sighted in, most rifles are remarkably reliable. But even the most accurate rifle can be "off" if it's knocked around enough.

34

Fighting
The Flinch

It's human nature to flinch at the anticipation of a high-powered rifle going off. It happens subconsciously, and even veteran hunters don't realize they're doing it. When you start squeezing that trigger, you know about when the rifle is going off and your subconscious doesn't like what's about to happen—loud noise and recoil.

When you flinch, the shot doesn't go exactly where you wanted it to go. The shot goes right, left, up, or down, depending on how you flinched. I know about flinching because I used to flinch; and my son, Jackie, used to flinch when he was learning to shoot a rifle. You could see his eyes squint

One way to fight flinch is to have a buddy load your rifle with spent and live shells; that way you never know whether you'll be receiving recoil or not. This will teach you to squeeze the trigger.

when he started squeezing the trigger. He was anticipating the kick and the noise rather than concentrating on putting the bullet where he wanted it.

Fight the flinch by taking a buddy to the range. Let him load the rifle for you. Along with your live ammunition, give him some empty cartridges. Don't look when he loads the rifle, so you won't know whether a live cartridge or an empty one will be in the chamber. This exercise teaches you to *squeeze* the trigger, which is critical for accurate shooting. If you jerk when you anticipate the shot, you've got a problem.

I learned about follow-through by playing competitive sports. Any sport you play has a follow-through, and my follow-through in shooting is to squeeze the trigger and keep my eye in the scope and my head still. The recoil may push me away from the scope, but I want to mentally feel as if I'm still looking through the scope. When I'm ready to shoot, I take a deep breath, let half of it out, squeeze the trigger, then keep my head down and try to maintain the sight picture. Ideally, you should be concentrating so hard on maintaining the sight picture that you're surprised when the gun goes off.

35

Perfect Practice Makes Perfect

There's an old saying that practice makes perfect. Wrong! Perfect practice makes perfect. You can take a golfer or tennis player who's been playing for 25 years, and he may be practicing four or five hours a day, but if he's practicing the wrong mechanics, he's not getting any better. Practice the proper mechanics to lock in muscle memory, do it correctly day in and day out, and you'll be successful.

The same principle applies to deer hunting. Practice shooting at the ranges you expect to shoot a deer. Don't just shoot at a paper target at 100 yards. Shoot at 200, 300, 400

When practicing with your bow or rifle, use 3D targets placed at different ranges and angles. Shoot from a treestand if at all possible.

yards. If you might shoot a deer that far, then practice shooting that far.

Shooting off a bench rest at a paper target is better than no practice at all, but you should practice shooting like you'll be shooting in the field. If you hunt on the ground, practice shooting from the ground. I hunt from treestands, so I practice shooting out of a treestand, using a 3-D deer target placed at different angles and different ranges. I practice like this with my bow and with my rifle. When I practice with my rifle, I tape a paper target over the target deer's vitals so I can see where the bullet hits. I try to practice shots at all the angles that I might shoot from when actually hunting.

I practice shooting from the same type of stand I hunt from, which helps me learn what shooting positions work best for me and which positions I should avoid. This, in turn, really pays off for me in hunting season.

36

Give It a Rest

For accurate rifle shooting, there's no substitute for a solid rest. If you don't believe me, just try shooting three shots at 100 yards from a bench rest. Then take three offhand shots at the same target. If you've never shot at a target without a rest, you'll be amazed at how much harder it is.

If you hunt on the ground, use a bipod that attaches to the fore-end sling swivel on your rifle. I use a bipod that swivels and has adjustable legs so I can shoot from a sitting or prone position. It makes a terrific rest for making a long shot on the ground.

I like to use an API treestand with a rifle rest. When you hunt from a box blind, the windowsill becomes your rifle rest. If you sit on the ground without a bipod, rest your elbows

For accurate shooting, a rest is critical. This hunter is using a bipod.
Credit: Ray Sasser

on your knees or get prone with a backpack for your rest. Otherwise, use whatever's handy—lean against a tree or a fencepost, anything to steady the rifle.

One trick I've learned is that a solid elbow rest is almost as important as the rifle rest. I'm left-handed, so I need a solid rest for my left elbow. A right-handed shooter would need to rest his right elbow against something. If there's no other alternative, jam your elbow in against your side. The last thing you want is a floating elbow.

When I get into a stand, I think about all my options. Where is the deer going to be when I shoot, and how am I going to get the best possible rest to make the shot? You can't wait until a deer shows up to figure out what you're going to do because the deer may not give you enough time. Squeezing the trigger is the easiest thing in deer hunting. Getting into position to make an accurate shot without a deer seeing or hearing you is much harder, requiring thought and preparation.

37

The Perfect Shot

In taking between 200 and 300 whitetails in my lifetime, I've tried just about every shot you can take. In my mind, there's no better place to shoot a deer than behind the shoulder. Whether I'm shooting an arrow or a bullet, I'm trying to get both lungs. If I'm successful, the deer dies quickly and humanely, and it doesn't run far before going down. With a lung shot, there's usually a pretty good blood trail to follow.

If you shoot in the crease behind the deer's shoulder, you've centered the lungs. The best thing about the lung shot is the margin of error. You're looking at a vital area roughly the size of a 12-inch circle. If you miss low, you hit the heart.

Jugular vein
Lungs
Heart
Liver

Illustration shows spots to aim for from various angles.

Miss a little forward and you hit the shoulder. Miss high and hit the spine.

Of course, not every shot is a perfect broadside shot. On a quartering-away shot, I try to aim so that my bullet or arrow strikes the offside shoulder. Otherwise, the penetration into the body cavity may be too shallow. If the deer is quartering toward you, a rifle shot on the leading edge of the front shoulder will take out both lungs and possibly drop the deer in its tracks. Shooting at a 3-D target is a good way to become familiar with the best angle for quartering shots.

If the deer is facing you head on, you can take him with a rifle shot in the middle of the brisket, just below the base of the neck. To make this shot, however, you need a steady rest and a short distance to the deer. Bowhunters must be more selective than gun hunters, but all hunters should know their limitations. I've passed up a lot of deer because I didn't feel good about the shot. When the deer is moving, or too far, or standing at the wrong angle, or I don't have a good rest, I'll pass up the shot.

38

Don't Miss High

Ninety percent of the shots missed at deer are high. If you shoot at a deer and he just stands there looking at you, chances are good the shot went high. When you get excited about taking a shot, you're more likely to jerk the trigger, and that makes the shot go high. When I aim at a deer with a bow, I aim at the lower one-third of my target area, which takes care of any tendency to shoot high.

Bowhunters talk about whitetails "jumping the string," which means they're reacting to the sound of the bow. I've learned about this the hard way because I've had a lot of bow shots go just over deer. I've looked at slow motion video of those missed shots, and the deer don't really jump when they

Aim your bowsight on the low side; that way, if the buck ducks down upon hearing the shot, you'll still hit the vital area. *Credit: Chris Armstrong*

"jump the string." They react to the sound so quickly that they duck down and turn to run, and the arrow misses high.

By putting my bowsight on the lower one-third of the deer's lungs, it will usually be a good shot, even if the deer ducks before the arrow gets there. If the deer doesn't react to the sound, I'm still in the vital zone by aiming low, and my exit wound is lower in the deer's body so I'm more likely to have an immediate blood trail.

If you're hunting with a shotgun, there's even more of a tendency to shoot high because most shotguns don't have nearly as crisp a trigger as a rifle. By comparison, it takes a pretty good pull to make the shotgun go off, and you wind up shooting high.

Even if they're shooting a rifle with a good trigger, hunters tend to shoot high because they misjudge the range and feel as if they have to hold over the deer so the bullet will drop in. Most of the time, the deer is not as far as they think. You should practice shooting at the longest distance you might shoot at a deer and find out for yourself how much your bullet drops at that distance.

When you're shooting at a deer, how do you know whether you're missing high or low? If you miss high with a rifle, most bucks will just stand there with no reaction whatsoever. If this happens to you, bring your next shot down. If you miss low, the bullet will usually hit in front of the deer, throwing up rocks, sticks, and other debris, and the buck will jump up in the air and take off in a hurry.

39

Medicine for Buck Fever

If you've watched the Buckmasters television series or Buckmasters videos, you know that I get excited when I get a shot at a good buck. When a big old buck comes along, I feel the adrenaline rush, and that's what makes deer hunting exciting. If I ever stop getting excited, it'll be time to quit.

You can't let that excitement turn into buck fever, because you'll start shaking so badly that you can't make an accurate shot. When I see that a deer is a shooter, it may register on me that he's a great buck, but I don't spend a lot of time counting points, estimating spread, and trying to decide how

Don't look at those antlers! Instead, concentrate on making the shot. You can look at the rack later! *Credit: George Barnett*

I'm going to have him mounted. If I were to do that, it would just get me more excited.

You should take the first good shot you feel confident about. I've had bucks coming to me at 100 yards and, with a rifle, I've just let them keep coming closer. You never know when the deer might smell you, hear you, change his mind, or get spooked by a coyote or distracted by a doe. I've lost some good bucks by not taking the first good shot they offered.

Rather than concentrating on how big the buck is, I concentrate on everything I have to do to make a good shot. From tennis, I learned that you play the game by making point after point. Points make up a game, games make up a set, and sets make up a match, so you concentrate on winning every point and let the rest of it take care of itself.

When I see that a buck's a shooter, I concentrate on my routine for making an accurate shot. That eliminates a lot of the mental stuff that causes buck fever. In every sport, including deer hunting, 80 percent of success is mental. I've had big bucks walking toward me, and had to watch them coming for a long way. If I feel myself getting too excited, I look away for a moment. Then I take three deep breaths to calm down, and concentrate on making a good shot behind the shoulder.

40

Looking
for The Eyes

If you can see a deer's eye, the deer can see you, and that's an important tip for a bowhunter to remember. When a deer is close, you cannot afford to move if he can see you. It's the movement that attracts a deer's attention and you, unfortunately, have to move in order to draw your bow.

I wait until the deer turns his head so I can't see his eye, or I wait until he walks behind a tree or bush so I'm certain he can't see the movement, then I draw. If the deer steps behind some cover, there's a timing issue involved in getting the shot because you can't hold a hunting bow at full draw for very long.

If you can see a deer's eye, he can see you. That's especially important to bowhunters, who can't afford to move in such a situation. *Credit: Ray Sasser*

If the deer stops behind cover and just stands there, you may have to let down the bow and wait for an opportunity to draw again. Along with stand placement that puts you in position to get the shot in the first place, knowing when to take the shot is a critical aspect of bowhunting. The deer has to be close before you draw the bow, and any sound or movement can give you away.

The ideal situation is for the deer to be moving steadily along a defined trail. When he walks behind a bush or tree, I draw. When he steps into an opening, I grunt to make him stop, then take the shot. It's hard to beat a broadside archery shot at a buck, so I try to set up my bow stand at a 90-degree angle and 20 yards from a game trail. If the deer's walking the trail, as I expect him to be doing, I'll have a broadside shot.

Experience is the best teacher in learning when to draw on a deer. Whenever you're in the woods, watch how deer move, even if it's a deer you're not planning to shoot. Even more than hunting with firearms, it's critical that a bowhunter take the first good shot the deer offers. While hunting, draw your bow on does and small bucks that you're not going to shoot, just for practice. Be careful not to spook them and ruin the rest of your hunt. This will give you confidence when your shooter buck finally comes.

41

Archery Mechanics

When you draw your bow, use the push-pull technique, pushing with the hand that holds the bow and pulling with your string hand. Keep the bow level when you draw. If you have to point the bow toward the sky in order to draw, you're pulling too much weight and you're making an extra motion that the deer is liable to notice.

One of the most common archery mistakes is gripping the bow tightly when you take the shot. I used to do this until Olympic gold medal winner Jay Barrs showed me how to shoot with my bow hand completely relaxed. The bow should

To shoot your bow accurately and consistently, have an anchor point and stick to it at all times. *Credit: Joe Songer*

be like a feather in your hand. You have to hold onto the bow until you start the draw, then you open your bow hand to form a horseshoe that cradles the bow.

If you grip the bow tightly, the torque causes the arrow to go left or right. Your bow should be equipped with a wrist strap that guarantees you won't drop the bow when you shoot.

A smooth release is critical, whether you use a mechanical release or fingers. I use a mechanical release and I concentrate on squeezing it just like a trigger. If you shoot with fingers, just relax your fingers and let go of the string—everything has to be smooth. Follow-through is important. Hold your form on the shot and don't drop your bow arm to sneak a peak at where the arrow is going. Keep your elbow up high with your draw arm. If your elbow starts coming down before your release, that's called "creeping," and it will throw your shot off.

Find an anchor point for your string and stick with it religiously. My anchor point is the top knuckle of my index finger touching my ear lobe. Yours may be the corner of your mouth. Practice that anchor point until you use it automatically. Repeat it in practice over and over until it's locked into your muscle memory. When it's time for the shot, your form should be so automatic that you don't have to think about anything but strategy. I use a Jennings bow. The short axle length makes it easy to use in a treestand or almost any hunting situation.

42

Peak Deer Movement

White-tailed deer move most during low light conditions. There are a lot of exceptions to this rule but, as a deer hunter, I try to be in my stand during the first two hours and the last two hours of the day.

A lot of factors contribute to deer activity, but I feel most confident about seeing deer early and late, particularly if I'm hunting deer going to or from a food source. If the food source is an open field, the deer will start leaving the field as daylight arrives. They may feed for a couple more hours in the cover as they trickle back to bedding areas, but they don't feel safe in the wide open during daylight hours.

Deer tend to move during low-light conditions, early and late in the day. The prime exception is during the rut, when bucks may be roaming about at any time. *Credit: Ray Sasser*

You get the reverse of that movement in the afternoon when the deer start showing up around food sources. Depending on weather, you may have deer feeding in open fields at midafternoon but they get more and more active as the sun drops and the light gets dimmer. We've seen the early-late phenomenon time and again. Our cameras are better now but, in the beginning days of Buckmasters, we passed up a lot of good bucks that came by our stands headed for bedding areas in the morning while it was still too dark to video or didn't show up in the afternoon until it was too dark.

About the only time I'll sit in a stand from daylight until dark is during the rut. When there's an active rut, you never know when something's about to happen. Of course sitting in a stand for nine or 10 hours is pretty tough. You really should hunt the way you enjoy hunting. If that means stand hunting for two hours in the morning and two hours in the afternoon, that's how you should do it. The key to enjoying deer hunting is to have a good time. Remember, you should have fun.

43

Be A
Weather Watcher

I'm a weather junkie, because knowing what the weather is going to do helps me predict how the deer will react. The first thing I do in the morning is turn on the Weather Channel and study the radar. Of course, the Buckmasters television crew hunts in all kinds of weather. When we travel to different locations around the country, we're stuck with whatever weather we've got, and sometimes we have to hunt on days when the weather is really awful. Because of those experiences, I probably know more about what type of weather deer don't like than what they do like.

Heavy snow will shut down deer activity for at least a full day. Make sure you're in the woods the next day though, because that's when deer will be on the move. *Credit Donald Jones*

I'm convinced that deer have an innate ability to sense weather changes. If there's a big cold front or a heavy rain coming, the deer will feed actively during the day because they know they may have to lay up for a couple of days. Conversely, if the weather is abnormally warm, deer become nocturnal.

One of the things I've noticed while hunting in cold weather is that a heavy snow will shut down deer activity for at least a full day. It seems to take deer almost 24 hours to get over the shock of a snowstorm. Make sure you're in the woods that next day, because the deer will be moving then.

The same thing happens with heavy rain. Deer don't seem to mind misty rain. In fact, they seem to like it. They don't like heavy rain, but they become active as soon as the rain lets up, and time of day doesn't seem to matter. If there's a heavy rain at sunrise that lasts until 11:00 a.m., then the deer will feed at 11:00 a.m..

Most hunters know that wind makes whitetails nervous, because heavy gusts make it harder for deer to pinpoint the source of smells. Everything is waving in the wind, and that makes it difficult for them to see danger too. Wind noise also makes it hard for deer to hear. I like to hunt in a steady 10 to 15 mph wind, because I can use the wind direction, and that steady breeze doesn't seem to spook the deer. I can also get away with a little more movement in my stand on a windy day as opposed to a calm day.

44

Mooning for Bucks

The truth is, I like to sleep. During my college days at Auburn, in fact, I was a member of the 14-hour club: I could sleep 14 hours at a stretch.

When I hunt on a full moon on my lease in Alabama, I see very little deer movement at dawn, when the deer are normally very active. Because of this, and despite the fact that it goes against the grain of what we generally do as deer hunters, I started sleeping late and going to my stand about 9:00 a.m.— a time when other hunters are often coming out of the woods. I used the full moon as an excuse to sleep late, and the tactic

During full moon phases, deer are more active at night; this in turn affects their daytime patterns. *Credit: Mike Searles*

worked! During a bright moon phase, I shoot a lot of deer between 9:00 a.m. and 1:00 p.m. Why? Well, assuming the
weather is good, deer are more active at night during a full
moon. That, in turn, alters their daytime patterns.

Another point to consider is that deer have a better
chance of seeing you when you're heading out to your stand
under a bright moon. People can see better on a bright moon,
but we don't have the kind of eyes that deer have. A deer's
eyes are made for seeing in low light situations; they can see
even better under the moonlight!

Traveling for Buckmasters, I've noticed the same full
moon influence from Canada to South Texas. When I travel to
a distant hunting hotspot for three or four days, I spend as
much time as possible in the woods because I have a limited
time to hunt. I have to! But when I'm hunting close to home
on a full moon, I do more midday hunting.

Even when I hunt during the early morning period on a
full moon and take a midday break, I try to get back into the
woods at least an hour earlier than usual for the afternoon
hunt. Deer seem to move earlier in the afternoons on a full
moon. A lot of calendars include moon phases, by the way,
and that helps when planning hunts. If I'm going to hunt in a
different state, for example, I consequently try to schedule the
hunt to coincide with a dark moon phase—which will give
more productive time in the woods.

45

After The Shot

I've seen white-tailed bucks run 100 yards or more with mortal wounds. Deer are incredibly tough, especially if they're flooded with adrenaline or pumped up by the rut. They'll run, even if they've been shot in the lungs or heart.

When I shoot a deer, I watch him run until he leaves my sight, and then I listen. A healthy deer running through the woods doesn't make much noise other than hoofbeats on the ground. An injured deer will crash into brush or trees and make a lot more noise. If you pay attention, you may hear the deer go down.

You can usually tell if the deer is hit by the way he reacts to the shot and the way he moves as he runs away. Every

The author pointing to blood on the ground, If you run out of blood sign, start making semicircle casts out away from where you found the last sign, and keep looking until you find the deer.

time you shoot, assume that you've hit the deer. It's important that you locate a good landmark—a rock or a tree where the deer was standing when you shot, or maybe the last place you saw the deer when he was running away. If you're shooting from a treestand or you're shooting a long distance across rough terrain, the place where you thought the deer was may not look the same once you walk to it.

When you find where the deer was, look for blood and tracks. They're easy to find in snow, but are tougher to find on rocky ground. If you locate the blood trail, follow it. If the trail is faint and it looks as if you'll have trouble finding the deer, stay off to one side of the trail so you don't mess it up. Mark the last place you find blood with orange ribbon or toilet paper.

If you run out of blood sign, start making semicircle casts out away from where you found the last sign and keep looking until you find the deer. If you know someone with a trailing dog, ask them to help you. We owe it to these animals to make every effort to recover them.

46

Approaching
Fallen Deer

Once you locate your fallen deer, approach carefully. Watch the deer closely for any signs of life. Whitetails are powerful, athletic animals and, while they're usually not dangerous to humans, a deer that's fighting for its life will hurt you. Just because a deer is down doesn't mean that it's dead. Deer that have been stunned can recover amazingly fast, especially if they detect your approach.

If the fallen deer has its eyes closed, watch out, because closed eyes mean the deer is still alive. I look for closed eyes and I watch to see if the animal is breathing before I approach. If there's any indication that the deer is still alive,

When you approach a downed deer, do so from behind, and stay ready to make a second shot. Watch to see if the animal is still breathing, or if its eyes are open or shut.

shoot it again. Under no circumstances should you approach a wounded deer and attempt to cut its throat. That's an invitation to get hurt, and it's more humane to dispatch the animal with another shot from a rifle, shotgun, or bow.

By the same token, if the deer is dead, it makes no sense to cut its throat and bleed out the carcass. Once the deer is dead, its heart is no longer pumping and all the bleeding has been done. If the deer is a trophy buck that you might have mounted, cutting the throat ruins the cape and causes problems for the taxidermist.

I always approach a fallen deer from the rear and I stay ready to make another shot. If something happens and the deer tries to run, it will run away from me and I won't get hurt. It's also easier to shoot a deer that's going away at close range than a deer that's coming toward you. If an injured deer is trying to escape, take any safe shot you can get. The idea is to bring the deer down and dispatch it with the least possible trauma.

As I approach a fallen deer, I poke it in the rear with my rifle muzzle or an arrow. If the deer is alive, you'll get a reaction when you touch it, but you'll be in a good position to make another shot.

Once you're certain the deer is dead, tag it immediately if you are on a tag system.

47

Shots For
a Lifetime

After you find your fallen deer and tag it in accordance with local game laws, take some photos so you can share them with your hunting buddies. It may take six months to a year to get a trophy buck back from the taxidermist. A c pact camera is another accessory that doesn't take up m space in your backpack. And a photo in the field looks better than a photo with the deer in the back of a truck, loa on a four-wheeler, or hanging from a meat pole.

Use paper towels or toilet paper to clean up as m blood as possible and make the photograph more appealin nonhunters as well as hunters. Either stick the deer's ton

Take along a camera for photos of your trophy: You'll be glad you did, and so will your friends. *Credit: R. Thornberry*

back in his mouth or cut off the tongue so it doesn't hang out in the picture. Try to pose the deer to show off his best qualities.

A low camera angle usually works best, particularly if you can pose the buck on the crest of a hill or a pond dam with blue sky behind the antlers. That really makes the antlers stand out. Try several poses with the deer to find the one that shows him off best.

If you shoot a buck late in the afternoon and plan to photograph him the next morning, you need to set him up so he stiffens with his head in an upright position and his front legs up under him. If you don't, he'll be difficult to pose after rigor mortis has set in.

When photographing a good buck, you should do everything possible to show the deer the respect he deserves. Don't sit on the buck or put your foot on him for the photograph. Taking good photos of a big buck requires some thought and work, but having good photographs is well worth the effort. When transporting your buck, try to avoid putting him on top of your car or truck. Don't leave your tailgate down or leave the deer uncovered on the back of your four-wheeler. If you can avoid offending nonhunters who might vote against us in the future, then do so.

48

Work Just Begins

There's an old saying that the work starts with a dead deer, and there's a lot of truth to that. Venison is excellent wild meat that's so low in fat it's often recommended to heart patients. Like any other game meat, however, venison tastes best when you take care of it properly in the field.

The first step is field-dressing or gutting the deer. Pack some latex medical gloves in your backpack and wear them for field-dressing, as it makes cleanup a lot easier. Field-dressing is not complicated and it basically involves removing all the deer's internal organs. That lightens the load by nearly

Once your deer is dead, the work is just beginning. Do an efficient and complete job of field-dressing, and you'll have tastier meals in the long run. *Credit: Ray Sasser*

20 percent, a big help when you have to drag or carry the deer or load it onto an ATV or into a truck.

The main thing to remember when you field-dress a deer is to avoid cutting into the paunch or intestines. Carefully make an opening in the abdomen, insert your middle and index fingers into the opening, put your knife blade between those two fingers, and use your fingers to keep the blade away from the paunch and intestines. Open the deer up from chest to pelvis, free the organs from the carcass, roll them out, and drain as much blood from the carcass as possible.

To get the best flavor from your venison, remove as much fat and connective tissue as possible. That's where a lot of the strong, wild taste comes from.

If you're hunting in cold weather, you can hang your deer outside. In the South, it's frequently warm during deer season and it's important that you get the deer to a cooler or locker plant as quickly as possible. If you have a long distance to drive, don't haul your deer in the open bed of a truck during warm weather or, worse, on the roof or hood. Keep the meat as cool and clean as possible.

49

Safety Sense

Contrary to what some people would have you believe, deer hunting is a very safe sport. The most dangerous part is driving to and from the woods. As an insurance policy to keep your hunting safe, it's a good idea to enroll in a hunter safety course. Most state wildlife agencies offer these basic education programs, as do the National Rifle Association and other firearms and conservation organizations. Many states require that you pass a hunter safety course in order to qualify for a hunting license.

Some veteran hunters may be grandfathered out of hunter safety requirements because of their age, but the courses are a good idea for anyone, regardless of age. If you have a son or daughter who's taking a hunter safety course, you

Especially if you have more than one big-game rifle, always check your ammunition before loading up. Too many cartridges look the same, on first glance. *Credit: Mark Wright*

should attend classes with them, both to support your kids and to monitor what they're learning. Most of us learned hunter safety from our grandparents, parents, or peers, and a refresher course doesn't hurt a thing.

Hunter safety is basically a matter of common sense. Never point the muzzle of your gun at anyone. Always make absolutely certain what you're shooting at before taking the shot, and be aware of the background and how far your shot might go if you miss the deer. When you're loading or unloading a firearm, walk away from your hunting partner and point your muzzle in a safe direction.

Treat every gun as if it's loaded. In fact, whenever you pick up a gun, be it your gun or someone else's, the first thing you should always do is open the action to see if it's loaded. When you're not actually hunting, it's a good idea to leave the action open so everyone can tell at a glance that the gun is safe.

Before shooting, double check your ammunition to make certain you have the right loads for that particular rifle or shotgun. I own a .270 and a 7mm Magnum, and I look closely at the cartridges to make certain I'm loading the right ammunition. If you use different caliber rifles during the season, never leave ammunition in the pockets of your hunting clothes. That's only inviting trouble.

Archery gear poses different problems and razor-sharp broadheads should be handled very carefully. Outfit your bow with a quiver that covers the broadheads. Don't try to climb into your stand while carrying a bow. After you're in the stand with your safety belt fastened, use a rope to pull your bow and arrows up to you. Lower them down with the rope before climbing down.

50

More
Safety Sense

Not all deer hunting safety involves firearms. You might have a heart attack in the woods or fall and hurt yourself. Every time you go out on a deer hunt, make sure somebody knows where you plan to hunt. It's best to hunt with companions, but that's not always practical or possible. Even if you don't hunt in established stands, leave someone a note or phone message saying that you plan to hunt east along Sandy Creek or south down the big draw.

That way, if you don't show up when you're supposed to, your friends will have some idea of where to start looking. Cellular telephones will work in a lot of places modern sports-